GETTING TO KNOW THE WORLD'S GREATEST
INVENTORS & SCIENTISTS

S T E P H E N

HAWKING

Cosmologist Who Gets a Big Bang
out of the Universe

WRITTEN AND ILLUSTRATED BY MIKE VENEZIA

CHILDREN'S PRESS®
AN IMPRINT OF SCHOLASTIC INC.
NEW YORK   TORONTO   LONDON   AUCKLAND   SYDNEY
MEXICO CITY   NEW DELHI   HONG KONG
DANBURY, CONNECTICUT

For Burt Joseph and Doug Welch: Thanks for helping me find my way through the universe.

Reading Consultant: Nanci R. Vargus, Ed.D., Assistant Professor, School of Education, University of Indianapolis

Science Consultant: Doug Welch, Ph.D., Professor, Department of Physics and Astronomy, McMaster University, Hamilton, Ontario

Photographs © 2009: age fotostock/Wojtek Buss: 18; Alamy Images/Helene Rogers: 27 bottom; AP Images: 30 (Paul E. Alers/NASA), 4, 5 (NASA/JPL-CalTech); Corbis Images/Bettmann: 19; Getty Images/AFP: 7; NASA: 24 (ESA/Hubble Heritage Team), 29 (JPL-Caltech/ESA/CfA), 25 (JPL-Caltech/K. Su (Univ. of Ariz.)); Photo Researchers/Emilio Segrè Visual Archives/American Institute of Physics: 3; Courtesy of Stephen Hawking: 10, 12, 16, 17, 21; Twentieth Century Fox Television/© 1990, *The Simpsons*™: 31; Woodfin Camp & Associates/Homer Sykes: 22, 23, 27 top.

Colorist for illustrations: Andrew Day

Library of Congress Cataloging-in-Publication Data

Venezia, Mike.
  Stephen Hawking : cosmologist who gets a big bang out of the universe/ written and illustrated by Mike Venezia.
       p. cm. — (Getting to know the world's greatest inventors and scientists)
    Includes index.
    ISBN-13: 978-0-531-23728-1 (lib. bdg.) 978-0-531-21337-7 (pbk.)
    ISBN-10: 0-531-23728-1 (lib. bdg.)   0-531-21337-4 (pbk.)
    1. Hawking, S. W. (Stephen W.)–Juvenile literature. 2. Physicists—Great Britain—Biography—Juvenile literature. 3. Black holes (Astronomy)—Juvenile literature. 4. Cosmology—Juvenile literature. I. Title.
    QC16.H33V46 2009
    530.092—dc22
    [B]
                              2008027650

All rights reserved. Published in 2009 by Children's Press, an imprint of Scholastic Inc. Published simultaneously in Canada. Printed in the United States of America.

Scientist Stephen Hawking, shown here when he was in his early thirties, is best known for his theories about black holes.

Stephen Hawking was born on January 8, 1942, in Oxford, England. Professor Hawking is a **theoretical physicist** and **cosmologist**. He has spent most of his life explaining how the universe began and why it behaves the way it does. Working with other scientists, he has come up with ideas that have changed our understanding of the universe.

Some of Stephen Hawking's most important work has to do with **black holes**. These are mysterious areas in outer space where **gravity** is so strong that anything that falls into them can never escape, including light! That's why they're called black holes.

In this telescopic photograph of the Milky Way, the white spot in the center is thought to be the site of a supermassive black hole.

Our own **galaxy**, the Milky Way, is thought to have a gigantic black hole near its center. This black hole is so large it could easily hold seven billion planet Earths. No one has to be concerned about the Earth getting trapped in this black hole, though. It's much too far away to worry about. Plus, most objects would orbit a black hole rather than fall into it.

Stephen Hawking is always coming up with new and interesting **theories** about the universe. A theory is a logical explanation for something that can be tested through experiments. Stephen and his scientist friends use mathematical formulas and information from modern-day telescopes to come up with theories that describe how the universe behaves.

What makes Stephen Hawking's story even more amazing is that he has done some of his most important work while dealing with a serious disease called **amyotrophic lateral sclerosis**, or ALS. He learned he had this disease when he was a young man. People with ALS eventually lose the use of all of their muscles. Stephen says he gets along just fine, though, and can do pretty much whatever he wants.

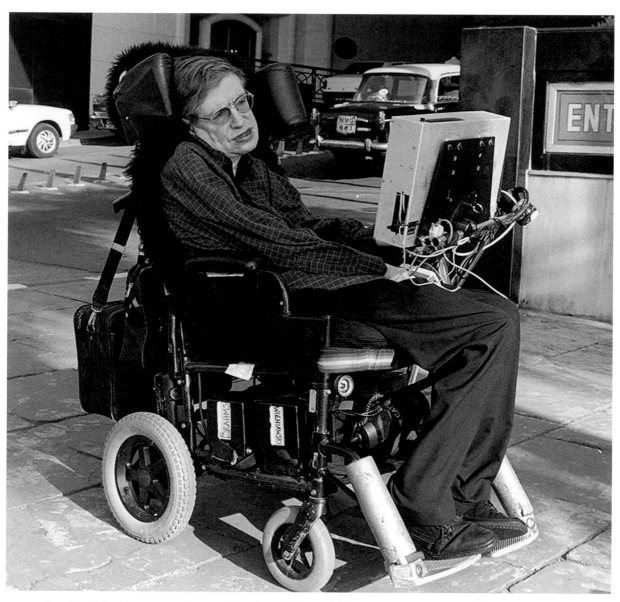

Stephen Hawking traveling in Mumbai, India, during an astronomy conference in 2001

Stephen Hawking grew up in an unusual family. At least friends and neighbors thought the Hawkings were unusual. Stephen, his two sisters, and his parents lived in a big old house near London. Mr. and Mrs. Hawking never seemed to mind if the paint and wallpaper were peeling, the roof leaked, or the carpets were worn through.

The Hawkings' creaky old house was filled with books, paintings, and odd items that

Stephen's dad had brought back from his
trips to Africa. Frank Hawking was a research
doctor who studied tropical diseases. Stephen
always looked forward to his dad returning
home with carved African animals, masks,
and other strange and awesome objects.

Stephen, shown here at the seashore with his sister Mary, had a happy childhood.

The Hawking house was a great place for adventure. Stephen discovered at least eleven different ways of getting in and out of the house undetected. One way was to climb up on the roof and enter through the window!

Mr. Hawking was the one who got Stephen interested in **astronomy**. On clear, dark nights,

Frank Hawking would get the whole family to lie outside and look up at the stars. Those experiences were the beginnings of Stephen's fascination with the universe.

Stephen did well in school. His friends and teachers had a feeling there was something different about him. Stephen was always full of ideas and energy. He enjoyed making up his own board games. One World War II game that he designed had over 4,000 pieces. Sometimes it would take weeks, or even months, to finish one of Stephen's games.

In 1958, for a high-school project, Stephen and his friends built a computer out of old electrical equipment and a used telephone switchboard. This was an incredible accomplishment for the time. It would be another thirty years before most people even knew what a computer was.

Stephen at about age twelve

When it was time to go to college, Stephen decided he would study **physics**, the science that deals with **matter**, energy, motion, and time. These were subjects that would help Stephen better understand the mysteries of the universe.

Surprisingly, though, Stephen had been totally bored with his physics classes in high school. It wasn't that the subject bored him. It was just that he knew more about physics than his science teachers and textbooks could teach him. In 1959, Stephen applied for a **scholarship** to go to Oxford University. He passed the difficult entrance test and was accepted to the school.

As he set off for Oxford, Stephen looked forward to learning everything he could about the universe. Unfortunately, even at Oxford, he soon became bored. The classes were too easy.

Stephen enjoyed pointing out textbook mistakes to his teachers. Instead of studying for exams, he spent time reading science-fiction books. He already knew the answers for all the tests!

Stephen (far right) was on the rowing team while at Oxford. He was the coxswain, the person who shouts out commands to control the direction of the rowing.

Stephen did have a good time at Oxford, even though he was bored with his classes. He joined the rowing team, went to parties, and made lots of friends. But during Stephen's third year, some of his classmates noticed that something was wrong with him. Stephen was getting clumsier. He fell over once or twice for no apparent reason. He once scared his roommates when he suddenly tumbled down a flight of stairs!

At first, Stephen pretty much ignored the warning signs that something was wrong with his health. He was more concerned about getting into the graduate program at Cambridge University. Cambridge had a great department of theoretical physics. Some of the best astronomers and cosmology researchers in the world taught there.

Now Stephen was forced to study. The entrance exam to get into Cambridge was much more difficult than the college exam he had taken to get into Oxford.

Stephen graduated with honors from Oxford University in 1962.

After graduating from Oxford, Stephen continued his studies at Cambridge University (above).

In 1962, Stephen was happy to learn he had been accepted to Cambridge. He hoped to get a Ph.D. there, the highest degree awarded by a university.

Meanwhile, Stephen was having more and more physical problems. When he returned home for Christmas break that year, his parents couldn't help noticing something was terribly wrong with their son.

Stephen was having trouble tying his shoes—and even holding a pen. His parents took him to the doctor. He then went through a series of tests. Finally it was discovered that Stephen Hawking had ALS, a disease that destroys the nerves that control a person's muscles. In the United States, this disease is sometimes called Lou Gehrig's disease, because New York Yankees baseball star Lou Gehrig had died from this illness.

In 1963, Stephen discovered he had ALS. In the United States, ALS is sometimes called Lou Gehrig's Disease, after the American baseball legend (right) who died of the disease in 1941.

Doctors told Stephen and his family that Stephen might live for only a year or two. Stephen became totally depressed. He didn't know if he would even live long enough to finish his **thesis**. A thesis is the important paper a student needs to write in order to get a Ph.D. Stephen began to realize that no matter how much time he had left, life was precious. He made up his mind to continue his studies and enjoy himself as much as he possibly could.

One thing that helped Stephen focus on life was meeting a girl named Jane Wilde.

Stephen met Jane Wilde while he was at Cambridge. This photograph shows them several years later.

Stephen and Jane met at a New Year's Eve party. Jane learned about Stephen's physical problems. She didn't seem to mind. Instead, she focused on Stephen's intelligence, energy, and remarkable curiosity about the stars and planets.

Stephen and Jane began to fall in love. Now Stephen felt he really had something to live for. He decided to work harder than ever on his thesis. After years of goofing off and being bored with his studies, Stephen found he was finally accomplishing something worthwhile.

Stephen and Jane Hawking with their children Lucy (in sandbox), Robert (standing), and Tim (on Stephen's lap)

Stephen and his sons play with a model of a black hole.

Stephen never complained about his disease. In fact, he began to enjoy life more than ever! In 1965, Cambridge University awarded Stephen a Ph.D. That same year, he and Jane got married. Stephen and Jane eventually had three children: Robert, Lucy, and Timothy.

And as time went on, it was clear that the doctors had been wrong about how long Stephen would live. No one knows why, but Stephen has lived many years longer than most patients with ALS.

Stephen finished his big thesis paper in 1966. It included mathematical explanations offering evidence that 13 billion years ago, the universe exploded into existence with a big bang. The Big Bang theory was already known, but Stephen's calculations showed exactly how it could have happened.

Other scientists around the world soon began talking about Stephen Hawking's amazing

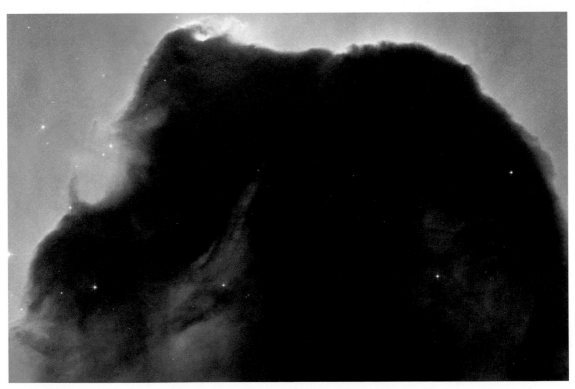

The Horsehead Nebula (above) and the Helix Nebula (opposite page) are gigantic clouds of dust, gases, and new stars. They are part of the universe, which Stephen Hawking and most other scientists believe was created by the Big Bang.

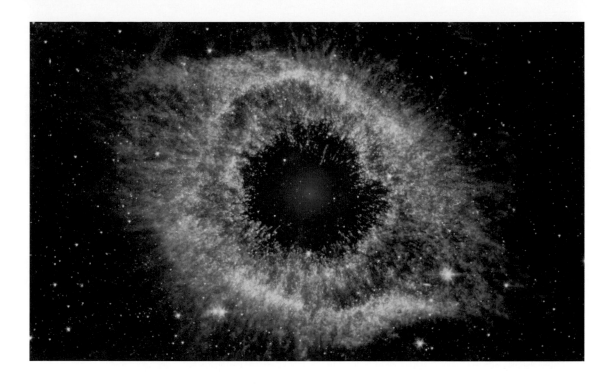

findings. This was the beginning of a great period of discovery for Stephen.

Unfortunately, over the next few years, Stephen's condition kept getting worse. As he gradually lost the use of his arms and legs, he went from using a cane to using crutches to using an electric-powered wheelchair. Things became even more difficult when, after an emergency operation in 1985, Stephen lost the use of his voice. So that he could continue to speak, he started using an artificial **voice synthesizer**. Today he operates the synthesizer by scrunching his cheek to move a stick that types words into a computer.

Even though Stephen's body wasn't doing very well, his mind was as sharp and clear as ever. Stephen kept coming up with new ideas and kept challenging old ones. Like any good scientist, Stephen changed his mind about certain things when new and better information came along that disagreed with some of his original theories.

Professor Hawking and students at Cambridge discuss mathematical concepts.

Stephen Hawking eventually became a professor at Cambridge. He often traveled the world giving lectures. He got around just fine with his electric wheelchair, computer, and voice synthesizer.

In 2001, things got a little easier for Stephen when he bought a brand-new, super-cool wheelchair called the Quantum Jazzy 1400 Power Chair. It was faster and more comfortable. As busy as Stephen was, he found time to help people understand strange and complicated scientific theories about the universe. Stephen began writing books, filming documentaries, and giving TV interviews to explain the wonders of outer space.

In 1988, Stephen Hawking published *A Brief History of Time*, a best-selling book that explained his theories about the universe in a simple way.

In 1973, Stephen Hawking had come up with some important findings that got a lot of attention. First, he showed that some matter actually could escape from black holes! This surprised many scientists, because it had been thought that nothing could escape from a black hole. Stephen explained how tiny **microscopic** particles of energy, called **quantum particles**, could escape. Stephen believed that over a long period of time, this loss of particles could cause a black hole to evaporate. He even described how a black hole would look as it faded away. This was a tremendous leap in understanding.

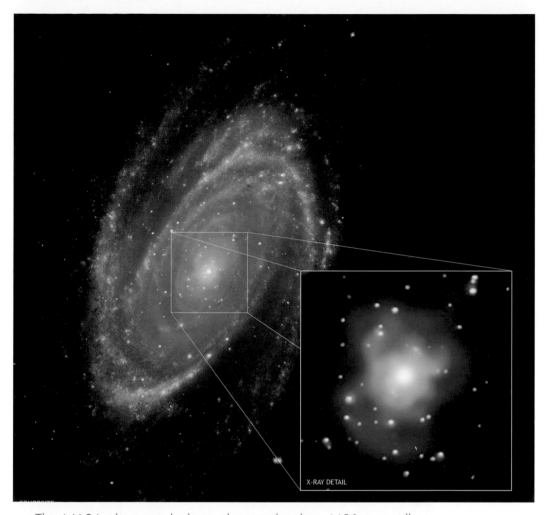

X-RAY DETAIL

This NASA photograph shows the spiral galaxy M81, as well as a close-up of the supermassive black hole at its center.

Scientists had been looking for a way to link their research on very large objects, like planets, stars, and black holes, to research on very tiny quantum particles. Stephen's theory showed how the two were connected. Today, Stephen's work on understanding escaping quantum particles is known as Bekenstein-Hawking radiation.

Stephen Hawking delivering a lecture on space

Stephen feels sure that sometime in the near future, cosmologists will find one theory that explains exactly how the universe got here and where it all came from. But one question Stephen thinks may never be answered is the biggest question of all: "Why does the universe go to all the bother of existing?"

With a talent for teaching and a good sense of humor, Stephen Hawking has opened the world of astronomy and cosmology to millions of people all over the world. As long as he is able, Stephen is dedicated to finding answers to the mysteries of the universe.

Stephen Hawking has a great sense of humor. In 1999, he made a guest appearance on the television show *The Simpsons*. It was his computer's voice that went along with the animated Stephen Hawking character.

Glossary

amyotrophic lateral sclerosis (uh-my-uh-TROW-pik LAT-uhr-ul sklur-OH-sis) A disease of the nerve cells that control muscle movement

astronomy (uh-STRON-uh-mee) The study of stars, planets, and space

black hole (BLAK HOHL) The area in space around a collapsed star where the star's gravity sucks in almost everything around it, including light

cosmologist (koz-MAHL-uh-jist) A scientist who studies the origin of the universe

galaxy (GAL-uhk-see) A very large group of stars and planets

gravity (GRAV-uh-tee) The force of attraction between massive bodies in the universe, including the attraction of objects toward the center of the Earth

matter (MAT-ur) Anything that has weight and takes up space

microscopic (mye-kruh-SKOP-ik) Too small to be seen without a microscope

physics (FIZ-iks) The science that deals with matter and energy

quantum particles (KWAN-tum PAR-tuh-kuhlz) Microscopic particles of energy

scholarship (SKOL-ur-ship) An award of financial aid offered by a college to a student

theoretical physicist (thee-uhr-RET-ih-kuhl FIZ-ih-sist) A scientist who uses mathematical models to explain how the natural world works

theory (THIHR-ee) A logical explanation, based on experimentation, that explains how or why something happens

thesis (THEE-siss) A written paper in which the author presents an idea or argument

voice synthesizer (VOISS sin-thuh-SYE-zur) An electronic device that can imitate the sounds of human speech

Index